CAMERAS. THERE'S ALWAYS CAMERAS

IT'S PART OF THE BUSINESS OF BEING A STAR.

YOU GET USED TO IT.

BUT SOMETIMES YOU JUST WISH THE CAMERAS WOULD DISAPPEAR.

CAMERAS IN YOUR FACE ARE PART OF THE JOB...

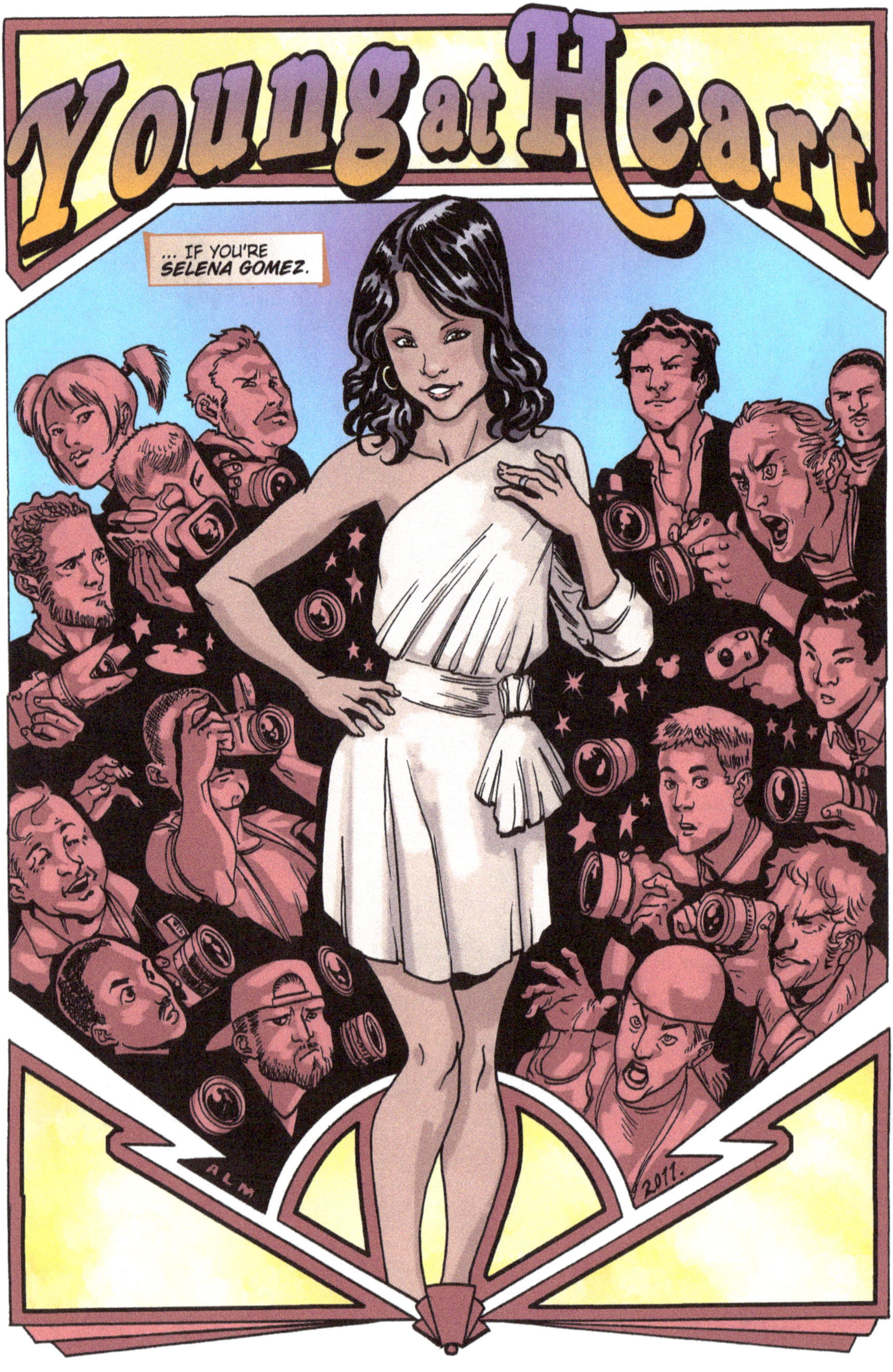
Young at Heart
... IF YOU'RE SELENA GOMEZ.
ALM
2011.

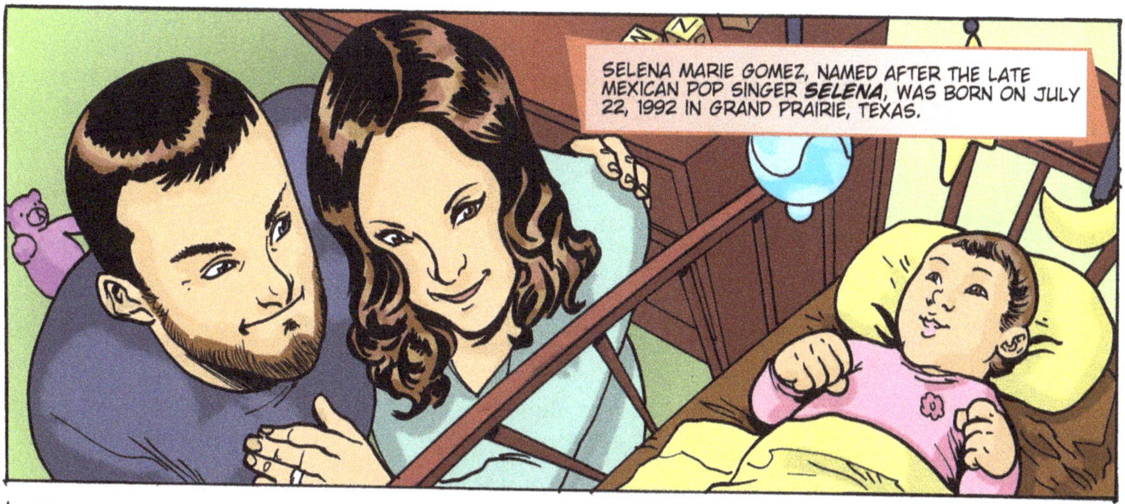
SELENA MARIE GOMEZ, NAMED AFTER THE LATE MEXICAN POP SINGER **SELENA**, WAS BORN ON JULY 22, 1992 IN GRAND PRAIRIE, TEXAS.

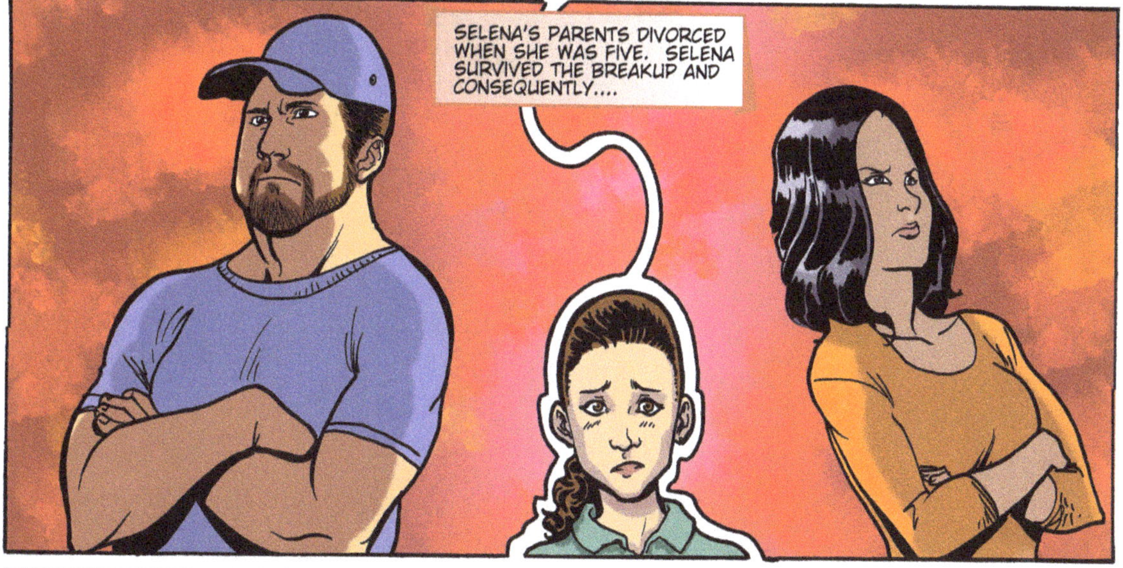
SELENA'S PARENTS DIVORCED WHEN SHE WAS FIVE. SELENA SURVIVED THE BREAKUP AND CONSEQUENTLY....

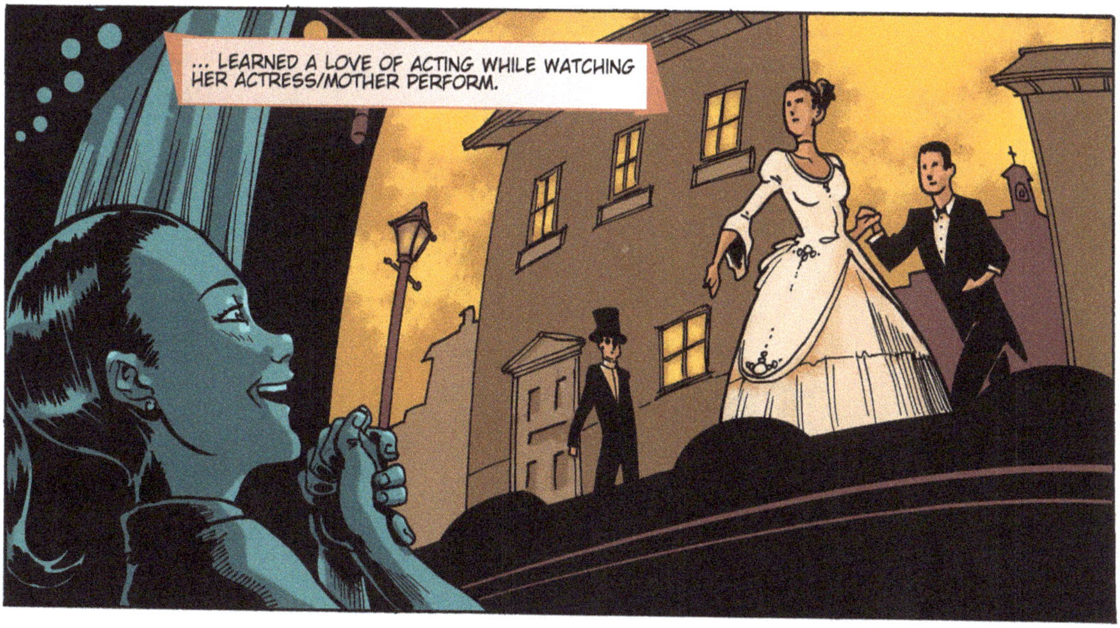
... LEARNED A LOVE OF ACTING WHILE WATCHING HER ACTRESS/MOTHER PERFORM.

SELENA BEGAN HER ACTING CAREER AT AGE 7 WITH A RECURRING ROLE ON THE CHILDREN'S TELEVISION SERIES *"BARNEY & FRIENDS"*.

SHE MADE HER MOVIE DEBUT AS *WATERPARK GIRL* IN THE 2003 FILM *"SPY KIDS 3-D: GAME OVER"*...

....AND IN THE ROLE OF JULIE IN THE TELEVISION MOVIE *"WALKER TEXAS RANGER: TRIAL BY FIRE"*.

BUT EVEN WITH A GROWING CAREER, SELENA REMAINED A DEVOTED CATHOLIC.

SELENA BEGAN WEARING A PURITY RING AT AGE 12, CONFIRMING HER VOW OF CELIBACY.

SELENA'S CAREER HAD NOT BLOWN UP YET AND SO SHE HAD TIME TO INDULGE HER FAVORITE PASTIMES; SKATEBOARDING, SURFING AND PLAYING WITH HER DOG. BUT HER FREE TIME WAS ABOUT TO DISAPPEAR.

DISNEY WAS LOOKING FOR THE NEXT *HANNA MONTANA* AND HAD BEEN CONDUCTING NATIONWIDE AUDITIONS.

THE TALENT HUNT ENDED WITH SELENA BEING SELECTED AS THE NEXT BIG THING!

DISNEY WASTED NO TIME IN GETTING SELENA IN FRONT OF THE CAMERA WITH A GUEST SHOT IN THE SECOND SEASON OF THE SERIES *"THE SUITE LIFE OF ZACK & CODY"*.

THE 2006 TELEVISION MOVIE *"BRAIN ZAPPED"* HAD SELENA DOING DOUBLE DUTY AS ACTRESS AND SINGER ON THE FILM'S TITLE SONG...

...BEFORE TAKING ON THE RECURRING ROLE OF MIKAYLA IN SEASON TWO OF THE HIT SERIES "HANNAH MONTANA".

IN 2007 SELENA WAS CAST IN THE DISNEY SERIES *"THE WIZARDS OF WAVERLY PLACE"*. THE SHOW WOULD RUN FOUR SEASONS AND SPAWN TWO MOVIES.

FORBES MAGAZINE NAMED HER ONE OF *"THE EIGHT HOT KIDS TO WATCH"*.

SELENA WAS SUDDENLY IN THE CELEBRITY LIMELIGHT...

A TIDAL WAVE OF OFFERS ROLLED IN...

...AND THE FUTURE LOOKED SO BRIGHT THAT SHE HAD TO WEAR SHADES.

ALM. 2011.

CONTRACT

SELENA DID DOUBLE DUTY IN THE MOVIE *"ANOTHER CINDERELLA STORY"*, CO-STARRING OPPOSITE TEEN HEARTTHROB DREW SEELEY AND SINGING THREE SONGS ON THE SOUNDTRACK ALBUM....

AND DID A MINOR VOICEOVER ROLE IN THE ANIMATED FEATURE *"HORTON HEARS A WHO!"*.

SELENA RECEIVED THE BEST POSSIBLE GIFT SHORTLY BEFORE HER 16TH BIRTHDAY, A RECORDING CONTRACT WITH *HOLLYWOOD RECORDS*.

IN 2009 SELENA AND FRIEND *DEMI LOVATO* RECORDED A DUET ON THE SONG *"ONE AND THE SAME"* FOR THE MOVIE *"PRINCES PROTECTION PROGRAM"*.

THAT SAME YEAR SHE SANG FOUR SONGS FOR THE WIZARDS OF WAVERLY PLACE SOUNDTRACK...

...AND A DUET WITH THE GROUP *FOREVER THE SICKEST KIDS* ON THE SONG "WHOA OH!"

SELENA BROUGHT TOGETHER A ROCKING BAND *THE SCENE* IN 2009 AND THE RESULT WAS THE GOLD ALBUM *"KISS & TELL"* AND THE PLATINUM SINGLE *"NATURALLY"* ...

...AND AN ELECTRIFYING LIVE TOUR, *"THE KISS TELL TOUR"*, THAT THRILLED AUDIENCES THROUGHOUT THE US.

A SECOND SELENA GOMEZ & THE SCENE ALBUM, "*A YEAR WITHOUT RAIN*", WAS EQUALLY SUCCESSFUL AS WAS A SERIES OF TRIUMPHANT CONCERTS THROUGHOUT 2010. SELENA TRULY HAD THE MAGIC.

SELENA WAS GROWING UP. AND AT AGE 17 SHE HAD HER FIRST ROMANTIC RELATIONSHIP WITH...

...NICK JONAS OF THE POP GROUP THE JONAS BROTHERS.

BUT THE CHALLENGES OF SEPARATE CAREERS KEPT THEM APART FOR LONG PERIODS OF TIME. THE COUPLE WOULD BREAK UP AND REUNITE SEVERAL TIMES OVER THE NEXT YEAR.

DURING THIS TIME, SELENA WAS FRONT AND CENTER IN SUPPORTING VARIOUS CHARITIES. THEY INCLUDED...

...AN APPEARANCE FOR THE ST. JUDE'S CHILDREN'S HOSPITAL *"RUNWAY FOR LIFE"* BENEFIT...

...SPOKESPERSON FOR *ISLAND DOG*, A DOG AID GROUP IN PUERTO RICO...

...AND THE ANTI VIOLENCE AGAINST WOMEN IN THE CONGO, *"RAISE HOPE FOR CONGO"*.

SELENA KEPT BUSY WITH A SERIES OF FILM AND TELEVISION PROJECTS THAT INCLUDED *"RAMONA AND BEEZUS"*.

SELENA AND NICK'S BUSY SCHEDULES RESULTED IN MORE TEXT TIME THAN FACE TIME AND...

...ULTIMATELY LED TO A PERMANENT BREAKUP IN APRIL 2010.

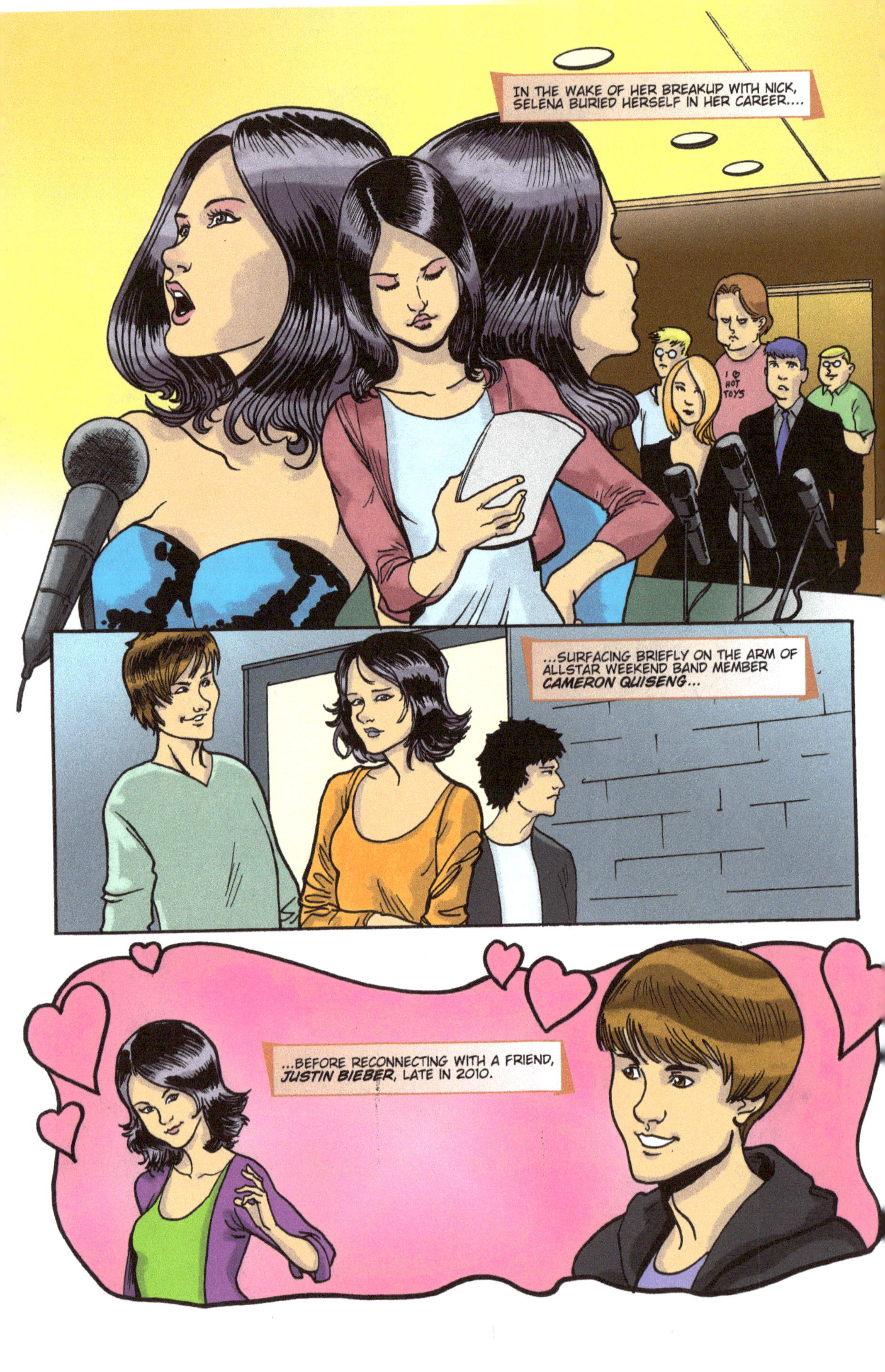
IN THE WAKE OF HER BREAKUP WITH NICK, SELENA BURIED HERSELF IN HER CAREER....
I ♡ HOT TOYS
...SURFACING BRIEFLY ON THE ARM OF ALLSTAR WEEKEND BAND MEMBER *CAMERON QUISENG*...
...BEFORE RECONNECTING WITH A FRIEND, *JUSTIN BIEBER*, LATE IN 2010.

BUT FRIENDSHIP QUICKLY TURNED TO ROMANCE WHEN SELENA AND JUSTIN WERE SPOTTED IN ROMANTIC CLINCHES ON A VACATION YACHT...

....LEAVING A MOVIE THEATER....

...AND COMING OUT OF A RESTAURANT AFTER A LATE NIGHT SNACK.

THEIR BUDDING ROMANCE HIT THE TWEETING AND TEXTING WORLD LIKE A GUNSHOT. AND THE FANS' RESPONSE WAS NOT GOOD.

SELENA RECEIVED COUNTLESS THREATS FROM *UPSET* JUSTIN BIEBER FANS. THEY UPSET HER SO MUCH THAT...

...SHE SAID "WE JUST LIKE TO HANG OUT AND THE TWITTERS CAN'T STOP US FROM HANGING OUT."

BUT IT DID FORCE THEM TO START SHOWING UP AT EVENTS SEPARATELY.

THE PAIR OFFICIALLY CAME OUT AS A COUPLE WHEN THEY WERE PHOTOGRAPHED WALKING HAND IN HAND ON THE SANTA MONICA, CA. BEACH PIER. WHERE IT ALL GOES AT THIS POINT IS ANYBODY'S GUESS.

HOWEVER SELENA HAD MORE GOING ON IN HER LIFE IN 2010 THAN A ROMANCE WITH JUSTIN BIEBER.

SELENA FORMED *JULY MOON PRODUCTIONS* AND WAS SIFTING THROUGH A NUMBER OF FUTURE PROJECTS FOR HERSELF.

SELENA AND HER BAND HIT THE ROAD EARLY IN 2011 FOR A HUGELY SUCCESSFUL US TOUR...

SELENA CEMENTED HER REPUTATION AS THE STAR ON THE HORIZON AS A PRESENTER AT THE *2011 GRAMMY AWARDS*...

...AND AS AN A LIST PARTICIPANT AT THE *PEOPLE'S CHOICE AWARDS* SHOW.

FAME

WHILE MOST 18 YEAR OLDS WERE GETTING READY TO BEGIN THE NEXT PHASE OF THEIR LIVES...SELENA HAD ALREADY LIVED NEARLY TWO DECADES OF STARDOM.

AND IT IS A SURE BET THAT THE STARDOM YET TO COME WILL BE MARKED BY...

...THE CLICK AND FLASH OF THE WORLD'S CAMERAS.

BLUEWATER COMICS

# FAME
## Selena Gomez

Marc Shapiro — Writer

Alex Lopez — Art

Steve Wands — Colors

Warren Montgomery — Letterer

Adam Ellis — Cover

**Darren G. Davis**
Publisher

**Jason Schultz**
Vice President

**Hayden Cowan**
Coordinator

**Jarred Weisfeld**
Literary Manager

**Kailey Marsh**
Entertainment Manager

**Maggie Jessup**
Publicity

**Janda Tithia**
Coordinator

**John Shableski**
Sales Director

**Atom Freeman**
Consultant

**Vonnie Harris**
New Business

**Steve Wands**
Graphics

**Jaymes Reed & Adam Ellis**
Logo Design

**Chad Jones**
Production

BLUEWATER COMICS

www.bluewaterprod.com

# PORTLAND'S

# CONCERT

# HALL

# TOC
## CONCERT HALL

www.ingramcontent.com/pod-product-compliance
Lightning Source LLC
Chambersburg PA
CBHW081235020426

42331CB00012B/3194